Firefighter

Lucy M. George

Ando Twin

Frank is a firefighter.
It's a very busy job!

When he arrives at work, he puts on his
special clothes and tests all the equipment.

"It's time for the fire drill!" Frank calls to his crew.

Everyone has a special job, so when there's an emergency they can work together quickly.

The alarm bell rings!

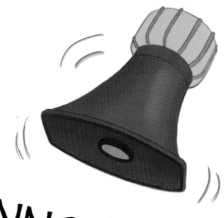

RRRIIINNNGGG!!!!

"There's a fire at the school," calls the watch manager.

Frank slides down the pole . . .

"GO!" he shouts.

And they are off!

At the school, there are bright flames
and smoke coming from the window!

The children are lined up safely in the playground.
The teachers are taking attendance
to make sure no one is inside.

Mr. Jones, the principal, points up at the window.

"The fire is in the library. Everyone is safe except Gerald the guinea pig. Please save him if you can!" he says.

Frank and his crew must get up to the library quickly!

The crew put on their masks to protect them from breathing in smoke.

Some of the crew attach the hoses to a fire hydrant while the others go into the school through the main door.

Frank climbs onto the turntable ladder on the back of the fire engine. It lifts him up high.

Frank looks through the window to check that it is safe to enter.

Then he carefully climbs inside.

There is lots of smoke in the library. The flames are bright red and very hot!

The rest of the crew rush
upstairs to help Frank.

"Point the hose there!" Frank shouts over the roar of the blaze.

The whole crew fight the fire in the library.

The children
watch from
the playground.

Finally, Frank comes to
the window and calls
down, "The fire is out . . .
and Gerald is OK!"

"Hooray!" the
children cheer.

An ambulance arrives to make sure that no one is hurt. The paramedics check the children and teachers, but everyone is fine.

The crew
make sure the school is
safe. They open windows
to help the smoke clear. Then
they put all their tools away.

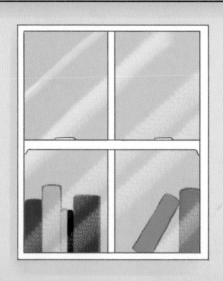

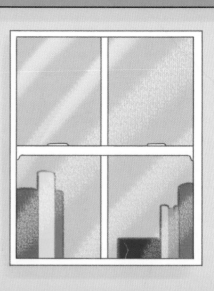

Frank is very happy because everyone did the right thing during the fire and no one was hurt . . . not even Gerald the guinea pig!

What else does Frank do?

Teaches people about fire safety.

Checks fire hydrants are working.

Rescues cats from trees.

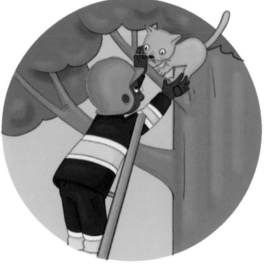

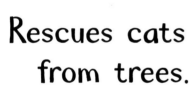

Helps people in road accidents.

Keeps fit and strong.

What does Frank need?

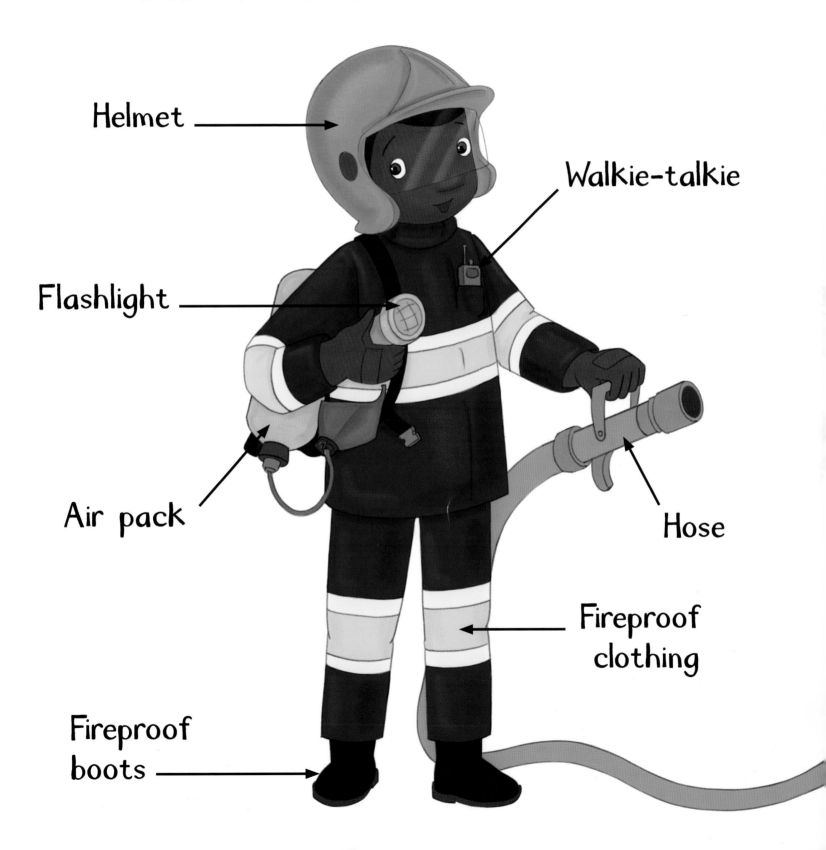

Helmet

Walkie-talkie

Flashlight

Air pack

Hose

Fireproof clothing

Fireproof boots

Other busy people

Here are some of the other busy people firefighters work with.

Paramedics help people at an accident and take them to the hospital if they are hurt. They carry medical kits and are specially trained to help people in an emergency.

Police officers sometimes come to a fire to help keep everything in order.

Call handlers answer 911 calls. They decide what kind of help is needed and sometimes stay on the phone until the emergency services arrive. They are trained to stay calm and speak clearly.

Watch managers send firefighters out to help people when emergency calls come in.

Next steps

- Discuss with your class what makes fire dangerous and why we should never play with it.

- What could cause a fire? Help children think of some things they can do to help keep a fire from starting.

- Have the children ever had a fire drill at school? Go over what the children should do during a fire drill.

- Do the children have any questions they might like to ask a firefighter? Make a list together.

- Have the children ever been to a fire station, or seen a fire engine? Plan a visit to a local fire station to learn more.

- Has a smoke alarm ever gone off at home? What happened? Ask the children to find the smoke alarms in their homes.

Publisher: Zeta Jones
Associate Publisher: Maxime Boucknooghe
Editorial Director: Victoria Garrard
Art Director: Laura Roberts-Jensen
Editor: Sophie Hallam
Designer: Anna Lubecka

Copyright © QEB Publishing, Inc. 2015

First published in the United States by
QEB Publishing, Inc.
6 Orchard
Lake Forest, CA 92630

www.qed-publishing.co.uk

A CIP record for this book is available from the Library of Congress.

ISBN 978 1 60992 829 2

Printed in China

For Granny Wilson
—AndoTwin

For Rose & Alex
—Lucy M. George